# Your Local Area
# RIVERS

**Ruth Thomson**

**Photography by Neil Thomson**

WAYLAND

First published in 2010 by Wayland

Copyright © Wayland 2010

Wayland
338 Euston Road
London NW1 3BH

Wayland Australia
Hachette Children's Books
Level 17/207 Kent Street
Sydney NSW 2000

Editor: Nicola Edwards
Designer: Edward Kinsey
Design Manager: Paul Cherrill

The author would like to thank Bridget Gibbs and
Alan and Pam Mawdesley for their invaluable Thames
boat trip.

British Library Cataloguing in Publication Data

Thomson, Ruth, 1949-
Your local area.
Rivers.
1. Rivers--Juvenile literature.
I. Title
551-4'83-dc22

ISBN: 978 0 7502 6086 2

Printed in China

Wayland is a division of Hachette
Children's Books.
www.hachette.co.uk

Free downloadable material is available to comple-
ment the activities in the Your Local Area series, including worksheets, templates for charts and photograph
identification charts. For more information go to:
www.waylandbooks.co.uk/yourlocalarea
<http://www.waylandbooks.co.uk/yourlocalarea>

# Contents

# What is a river?

A river is a broad stream of fresh, not salty, water. It is always on the move, flowing over the land in one direction only – downhill.

A river flows in a channel that it has worn away in the ground. The bottom of the channel is the river bed. The sides are called banks.

 **What difference can you spot between these two rivers?**

Rivers are part of a never-ending water cycle. Rainwater falls on land, soaking into the earth or running into streams. The streams join to become rivers, which flow into lakes or the sea.

## A local look

Clean, fresh water is precious. This chart shows how much water people use daily in different activities.

### Everyday water use

| activity | litres used |
| --- | --- |
| flushing the toilet | 8 per flush |
| bath | 60 |
| shower | 15 |
| drinking | 1 |
| car wash | 25 |
| washing up | 8 |
| dishwasher | 45 |

★ **Use the chart to work out how much water you use in a day or a week.**
★ **Can you think of ways to reduce your water use?**

When the sun shines, water evaporates, turning into invisible water vapour. The vapour rises high into the sky. It cools down as it rises and turns back into tiny water droplets. The droplets form clouds.

When they are too heavy to stay as clouds, the drops fall as rain, sleet or snow. The water cycle begins again.

# A river's course

Many rivers begin as rain falling on hills or mountains. The place where a river starts is called its source.

Trickles of water join together to form a narrow, shallow stream. This falls steeply and quickly downhill. The rushing water loosens pieces of rock and washes them away. These bump together along the river bed, breaking into gravel and sand.

rock worn smooth by rushing water

waterfall

rapids

The upper part of a river is often broken by waterfalls, where the water falls steeply over hard rock. There are also stretches of rapids, where shallow, fast-flowing water tumbles and foams around rocks.

everal streams join the largest
ne to form a river. As the land
attens, the river moves more
lowly. It widens and deepens.
ome loose gravel, mud and
and fall to the river bed.

A river ends when it reaches the sea.
This is called its mouth. By now, the
river moves very slowly and widens
into an estuary. Here, fresh river water
meets the salty sea.

The river no longer flows fast enough
to carry its load of mud, which it drops,
to form mudflats.

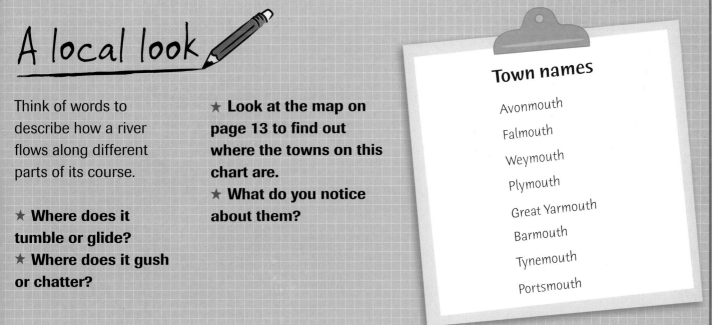

# A local look

Think of words to
describe how a river
flows along different
parts of its course.

★ **Where does it
tumble or glide?**
★ **Where does it gush
or chatter?**

★ **Look at the map on
page 13 to find out
where the towns on this
chart are.**
★ **What do you notice
about them?**

## Town names

Avonmouth

Falmouth

Weymouth

Plymouth

Great Yarmouth

Barmouth

Tynemouth

Portsmouth

# Shaping the land

Rivers wear away the land that they flow through and slowly change the shape of the landscape. This wearing away is called erosion.

In hilly land, the force of river water carves through the softest ground to make narrow, V-shaped valleys with steep sides.

In lowland areas, rivers wind their way in large bends known as meanders. The meanders gradually wear away the river banks.

? What shape does this river make?

Some meanders snake back and forth across a valley floor in enormous loops, to create a flat floodplain, like this one.

# A local look

Erosion happens on the outside of bends where water flow is faster. The water washes away loose soil and rock.

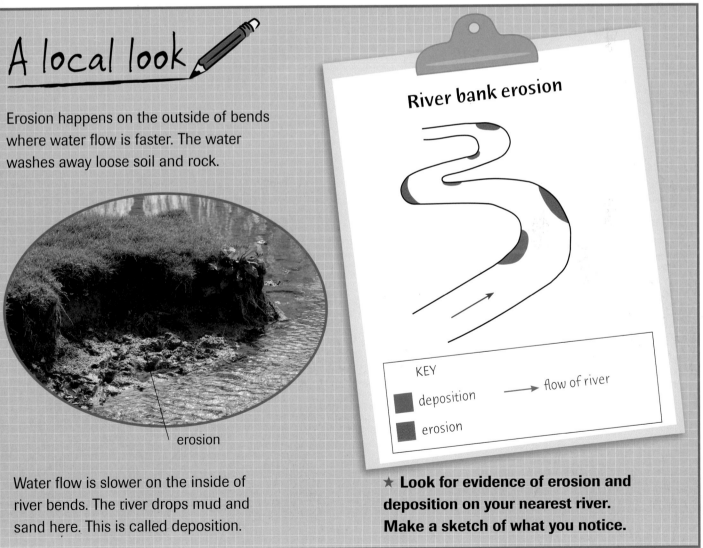

erosion

Water flow is slower on the inside of river bends. The river drops mud and sand here. This is called deposition.

## River bank erosion

KEY

deposition

erosion

→ flow of river

★ **Look for evidence of erosion and deposition on your nearest river. Make a sketch of what you notice.**

# Plants and birds

The water in hillside streams flows too fast for many plants to grow there. Trees, grasses and flowers that can live in waterlogged soil line slow-flowing rivers. Willow and alder are the most common trees. Their knotty roots help stop water washing away earth from the banks.

willow

common reeds

Tall reeds and rushes grow in dense clusters. Their tough, tangled roots grip firmly in the mud.

In summer, flowers appear on the banks and in calm water.

yellow flag iris

purple loosestrife

# A local look

Look out for water birds at different times of the year. Ducks, swans and geese are good swimmers. They all have webbed feet. Coots spend more time on land. Their feet are only partly webbed.

mallard drakes (male) and duck (female)

coot

Canada geese

★ **Notice what birds eat. Do they eat in the water, on land or in the air?**

★ **Do they dive for food or eat near the surface?**

mute swan and cygnets (chicks)

★ **Look out for nests on the water and for birds with their young. Young birds often look quite different from adult ones. Make sure you don't disturb them.**

coot chick on tyre nest

### Birds I have seen

| date | bird | place |
|------|------|-------|
| 10 June | swan | River Thames at Windsor |

Keep a record of the birds you see each time you visit a river.

# Where are rivers?

There are hundreds of rivers all over the United Kingdom. They flow to the sea in all directions – to the English Channel, the North Sea, the Irish Sea, the Bristol Channel or the Atlantic Ocean.

**?** Why were London and Bristol once important ports? Research your answer on the internet.

The Severn is the longest river in the United Kingdom and the River Thames is the deepest.

Bristol

The Thames flows through the centre of London.

# A local look

This map shows the longest rivers in the United Kingdom.

★ **Which is the nearest one to where you live?**

★ **Find out how long your nearest river is and whether it joins any other rivers.**

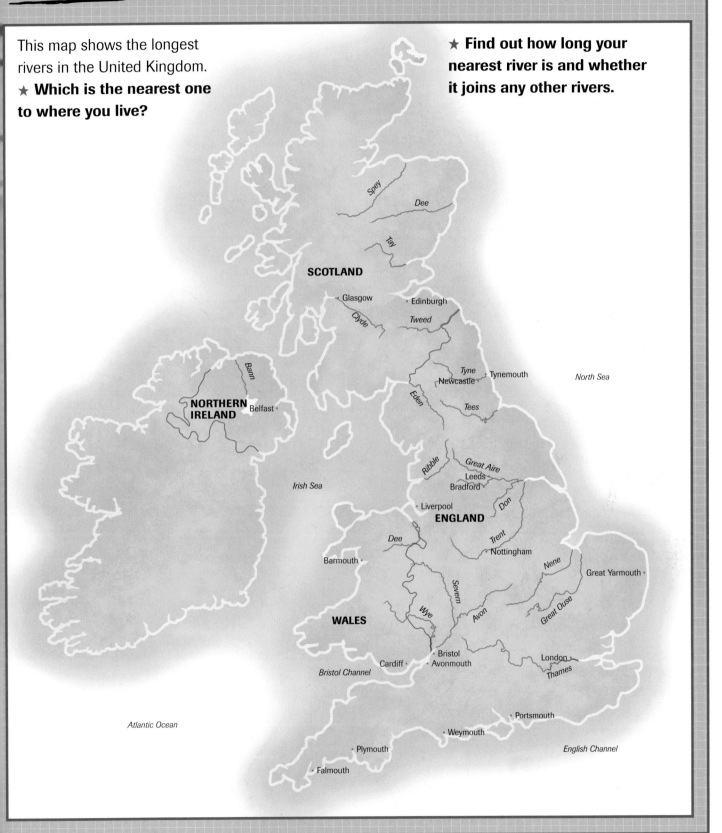

Spey

Dee

Tay

**SCOTLAND**

Glasgow • • Edinburgh

Clyde Tweed

Bann

Tyne

**NORTHERN IRELAND** Belfast • Newcastle Tynemouth *North Sea*

Eden Tees

Ribble Great Aire

*Irish Sea* Leeds Bradford

Liverpool • Don

**ENGLAND**

Dee Trent

Barmouth • Nottingham

Nene Great Yarmouth •

Severn

Wye Avon Great Ouse

**WALES**

Bristol • London •

Cardiff • Avonmouth Thames

*Bristol Channel*

Portsmouth •

*Atlantic Ocean* Weymouth •

Plymouth • *English Channel*

Falmouth •

# Follow a river

Rivers have played an important part in shaping sites for settlements and industries. Major towns and cities in the UK, including Newcastle, Liverpool, Bristol, Nottingham, Belfast, Glasgow, Leeds, Edinburgh, Cardiff and Bradford, are all on rivers or estuaries.

river crossing in Bath

Rivers also form a natural boundary. If you look on old maps, you can see how county boundaries often follow the course of a river.

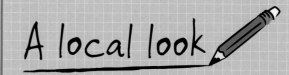

This map shows the course of the River Stour, in eastern England.

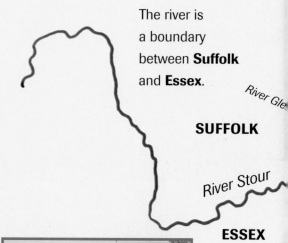

The river is a boundary between **Suffolk** and **Essex**.

River Gle

**SUFFOLK**

River Stour

**ESSEX**

Belchamp Broc

In the 18th and 19th centuries, barges came as far as **Sudbury** with heavy loads.

In the past, horse-drawn traffic paid to cross a bridge over the river at **Stratford St Mary**.

**Make a map of the course of your nearest river, from its source to the sea. Use an Ordnance Survey (OS) map to help you.**

★ **Mark towns and villages on the river as well as features, such as big bridges.**
★ **Find out if any famous person, building or event is connected with the river.**

John Constable, a famous British artist, painted many pictures of the river and the lock near **Flatford Mill**.

Many old warehouses at the docks along the river have now been turned into flats.

• **Sudbury**

River Box

River Brett

*River Stour*

ambridge Brook

**Stratford St Mary** •

• **Flatford Mill**

*River Stour*

**Mistley Quay** •

**Felixstowe** •

**Harwich** •

*NORTH SEA*

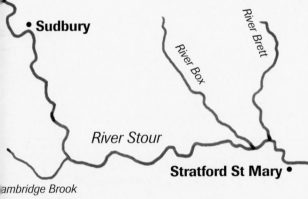

Several freight ships land cargo at **Mistley Quay** every week.

Passenger ships sail from **Felixstowe** and **Harwich** to Germany, Holland, Denmark and Belgium.

# River crossings

People need ways to cross rivers and streams. Long ago, they crossed at shallow places, called fords, on foot or on horseback.

ford

They crossed wider rivers by boat. Ferries still take people across several river estuaries.

16

## A local look

Many towns grew up around fords or bridges and are named after them. Stratford, Bradford, Cambridge and Tonbridge are examples.

**Flatford** >

THE DICKER — 1¼
HORSEBRIDGE — 2
HELLINGLY — 3¾

Some places have a name ending in -brook, -burn, -bourne or -beck. These are all other names for a stream.

★ **Look on a road atlas and list as many places as you can named after river crossings.**

### Places named after river crossings

Welbeck

Hereford

Edenbridge

Bannockburn

Bridgewater

Fordingbridge

Colebrook

Duntisbourne

ventually, people built bridges, sually of stone, but sometimes f wood, brick or, more recently, concrete.

19th century painted cast-iron bridge

 **What material is the bridge over your nearest stream or river made from?**

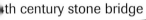
th century stone bridge

wooden footbridge

modern concrete bridge

## SIGN OF THE PAST

In some places, people had to pay a fee called a toll to cross a bridge. Some tollhouses, where the toll collectors lived, still survive next to bridges.

# Rivers in the past

Before lorries and railways were invented, the best way to transport goods across the country or overseas was by boat. Dockers loaded the goods from platforms called wharves. They stored goods waiting to be shipped in warehouses on the quay.

River water turned waterwheels that powered factory machines for making cloth, paper and iron. Waterwheels also powered millstones that ground grain into flour.

**?** **Why does a waterwheel have ridges?**

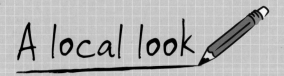

★ **Find names on old buildings that tell you how these were once used.**

★ **Look near a river for street names that give you a clue about their history.**

This sign is a clue that dockers at this wharf dealt with goods from countries surrounding the Baltic Sea, such as Germany, Sweden, Finland and Poland.

Builders have converted many disused wharf warehouses into homes, offices, cafés, shopping malls, museums or galleries.

★ **What features have the builders left to show how these buildings were used in the past?**

Cranes were used for loading and unloading heavy goods. You can sometimes still see these on quaysides.

# Canals

More than two hundred years ago, mine and factory owners built artificial waterways, called canals. These linked rivers or provided new waterways for transporting goods from places without a nearby river.

Soon there was a canal network all over the country. Barges carried heavy loads of coal, wood and stone or fragile goods, such as pottery.

Canals were built along the straightest possible route. They went in tunnels through hills and in aqueducts across valleys. Locks took canals up and down hills. A lock raises or lowers boats from one water level to another.

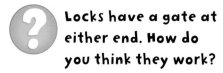

**?** Locks have a gate at either end. How do you think they work?

By Victorian times, there were railways all over the country. Railways were faster and cheaper than canal barges and could carry more heavy goods at once. Canals fell into disuse. Now many have been cleaned and restored. People travel along them in narrowboats for pleasure.

Horses once walked along the towpaths beside canals, pulling the barges. Cobbles like these stopped horses from slipping backwards on slopes.

narrowboat

# A local look

★ **Where is your nearest canal? To find out, check at www.waterscape.com**

| Walthamstow Marshes | 1 ½ miles |
| Old Ford Lock | 4 miles |

| Pickett's Lock | 3 ¼ miles |
| Enfield Lock | 6 ¼ miles |

★ **Research in your local library or on the internet to discover why the canal was built, what goods were carried along it and where they went.**
★ **Find out what old buildings beside the canal were once used for.**

# Work

In the past, thousands of people worked on boats or at ports. Modern container ships are too big for docks built 100 years ago. They need deeper water and special equipment for loading and unloading. Some docks have become marinas for pleasure boats instead.

marina

dredger

There are still jobs to do on rivers. Dredgers scoop out silt from riverbeds, to make the water deep enough for boats. Some workers make sure river water is clean or clear up oil spills or manage rivers to help protect river wildlife.

A local look

★ **Find out what jobs people do on or beside rivers.**
★ **Write a description of one of the jobs.**

boat building and repairs

lock keeper

Ferry operators take people from one place on a river to another. Other people have jobs taking tourists on sightseeing round trips.

 **What similarities can you spot between these two passenger boats?**

Fire and rescue service boats are equipped to help anyone who is in difficulty on the water or who needs rescuing from a flood. The crews are trained in first-aid.

# River fun

There are all sorts of leisure activities that people can enjoy by rivers. Some people like strolling or cycling along riverside paths or fishing from the banks.

Other people prefer to go out in boats – rowing, sailing, canoeing or motorboat cruising, or taking river trips.

**?** Why does this boat have lifebelts fixed on the front?

## A local look

★ Which of these river activities are noisy and which are quiet?
★ Which activities are active and which are relaxing?
★ Find out what activities people do on your local river.
★ Which activities might:
  – damage the riverbanks?
  – pollute the water?
  – disturb wildlife?

walking

fishing

ainting

kayaking

motor boating

cycling

feeding birds

ailing

rowing

# Dirty rivers

Rivers are not always very clean. Litter, especially plastics that do not rot, can wash into the water from the banks. After storms, sewers can fill up quickly. The overflow runs into rivers.

**?** What kind of pollution can you see in this picture?

Farmers use fertilisers to help crops grow. Rain may wash these chemicals into rivers. Both sewage and fertilisers encourage algae to grow and reduce the amount of oxygen in the water. Without enough oxygen to breathe, fish and other water wildlife die.

algae

# A local look

★ Take photographs of any evidence you find of river pollution.

★ Send the photos with a letter to your local river authority. Remember to say where you took the photographs.

detergent

dead fish

litter

Think of ways you could take care of your local stream or river.

★ Could your class 'adopt' a stream to keep clean?
See www.ukrivers.net to find out how.

★ Make a poster reminding people not to leave litter on river banks or throw rubbish into the water.

Poster designed by D.J. Royal, Age 10, George's Primary School, Bristol

# More things to do

Make a study of a local stream throughout a year.
★ Sketch what grows along the banks and in the water in each season. Identify the plants in a flower book.

Choose a riverside tree to record over different seasons.
★ In winter, study its twigs, bark, buds and tree shape.
★ In spring, look at its flowers and leaves.
★ In autumn, look at its fruits. Sketch or photograph them all.
★ Notice whether any birds visit the tree to find food.

A stream can be unexpectedly deep. Test its depth with a measuring stick first before you wade in. Banks can be slippery, so be careful where you tread.

### The common elder

**February**
Catkins start to lengthen.

**March**
Catkins turn yellowy green when they flower and shed pollen.

**April**
Leaves appear.

**October**
Fruits ripen and release seeds.

**November**
Leaves fall off.

**November - March**
The empty cones stay on the tree.

Compare the depth, width and speed of the water at different times of year.
★ Mark out a 10m section of stream. Drop a twig or a rubber ball at one end. Time how long it takes to reach the other end. Divide the number of seconds by ten to calculate the water speed in metres per second.

esearch the history of a bridge over your local ver, or find out about one of these famous bridges.

**Iron Bridge** at Coalbrookdale was the world's first ast-iron bridge.

**The Clifton Suspension Bridge** in Bristol was esigned by Isambard Kingdom Brunel.

**Tower Bridge** in London can be raised to let boats ass through.

**The Severn Bridge** crosses the Severn river between ngland and Wales.

**Pulteney Bridge** in Bath is one of only four bridges the world lined with shops on both sides.

**The Humber Bridge** over the Humber Estuary is more han 2.2km long.

**The Forth Rail Bridge** over the Firth of Forth in cotland was the world's first major steel bridge.

**Monnow Bridge** has a gatehouse on it, where oldiers once guarded the entrance to Monmouth.

**Gateshead Millennium Bridge** spanning the River yne is only for pedestrians and cyclists.

Tower Bridge in London

Pulteney Bridge in Bath

★ **Design a signpost for your local river, giving it a watery feel.**
★ **Design a bench to put on a nearby riverbank. Think of a suitable theme, such as boats, wildlife or a local industry of the past.**

# Glossary

**algae** tiny green plants. Most of these live in water

**bank** the side of a river

**canal** an artificial waterway

**channel** the river bed and banks that contain a river

**container ship** a large cargo ship designed to carry truck-sized metal boxes, called containers

**course** the path of a river

**dredging** digging out mud from a river bed

**erosion** the wearing away of rock and soil by water, wind or ice

**estuary** the widest part of a river where fresh water meets the sea

**evaporate** when a liquid changes into gas by heat

**fertiliser** chemicals that some farmers add to the soil to help crops grow

**floodplain** the broad, flat area of land in a river valley that often floods. The mud left behind after a flood makes the soil very fertile

**lock** a way of raising a boat from one water level to another

**meander** a large natural bend in a river

**mudflat** the area of mud at a river's mouth that has been washed downstream

**narrowboat** a boat used on canals, built to fit into the narrow locks

**pollution** when air, water or land is harmed, spoiled, damaged or poisoned

**rapids** a steep, shallow, fast-flowing, rocky stretch of a stream

**river bed** the bottom of a river

**silt** fine particles of sand and rock

**source** where a river begins

**stream** a small river

**Victorian** the time when Queen Victoria ruled Britain – from 1837 to 1901

**waterfall** a place where a stream or river falls over a steep drop

# ❓ Talking points

The questions in the book encourage close observation of the pictures and provide talking points for discussion.

### Page 4
Rivers cut their own channel through the land. However, over time, people have changed the course of some rivers. They may have straightened and strengthened the banks, as in the bottom picture, where modern houses line the bank. Trees and plants line the banks of the river in the top picture. These will probably still be trimmed and managed.

### Page 7
Ask children as a group to list words comparing a stream with a river. Compare the way both move; the sounds they make; the feelings children might have if they were standing in trickling, rushing or calm water. The list of words could be used to create concrete poems in the shape of a river from its source to the sea. All the town names listed are by the sea, at a river's mouth. Ask children if they can follow one of the rivers back to its source on an atlas or a map.

### Page 8
Rivers never flow in a straight line. In the hills, the entire valley bends from side to side, like a snake, as the river cuts its course.

### Page 11
Ask children to research what features birds have that are adapted for a watery environment. Ducks have waterproof feathers, wide bills for filtering food from the water's surface and webbed feet. Herons have a long neck and long sharp beak for catching fish.

### Page 12
Children might like to investigate the history of their nearest seaport, such as Liverpool, Glasgow or Belfast, or an inland port such as Gloucester. What was it once like? Where has the port moved to? What has happened to the old dock buildings? Children could look up container ships, bulk carriers and super tankers on the internet to find out why some ships cannot dock in old ports.

### Pages 14-15
Researching their nearest river is an opportunity for children to develop map skills. You may need to use maps with different scales. This project also offers an opportunity to research local history and even to interview members of the wider community.

### Page 17
• Children might like to research and collect pictures of different types of bridges, for example, simple slab and clapper bridges, arch bridges, cantilever bridges, suspension bridges, beam bridges and bascule bridges (such as Tower Bridge) and identify their differences.

### Pages 18-19
• Waterwheels have ridges that fill with or scoop up water and make the wheel turn.
• When builders convert old docks they often leave the original hoists, windows and doors and signs, but clean up the brickwork and sometimes add balconies. Children might like to discuss why doors and windows are the shape they are and how a hoist worked.

### Pages 20-21
• There are several organisations and a number of canal and waterway museums that provide comprehensive information about the working of canals and locks, their history, their geography and their future:
www.britishwaterways.co.uk
www.canalmuseum.org.uk
www.stokebruernelocks.com

### Pages 23-25
• Both passenger boats are designed with seating for a large number of people. They have a covered cabin for shelter in wet or windy weather and an open-air seating area as well. All passenger boats have life rafts, in case they overturn and people need help in staying afloat in the water.
• All human activities have the potential to change a river and its banks. Walking and cycling can wear away the banks and people can spoil banks with litter or by picking or trampling on plants. The wash from motorboats can damage the banks as well as disturbing wildlife with their speed and noise. Children could discuss how best to balance people's enjoyment of rivers with the need to conserve the environment.

### Pages 26-27
• Litter and sewage pollute the river in this picture.
• www.environment-agency.gov.uk provide useful educational materials about keeping rivers clean.

# Index